I0168778

BODY POLITIC

Poetry by Rich Murphy

Published by Prolific Press Inc.
Johnstown, PA

Printed in the USA

Acknowledgements: *Aji:* "As Enfolded in a Blanket;" *Backlash Journal:* "Lullaby for a Lullaby;" *BlazeVox:* "Across a Nation," "Notes from the Margin," "Not (only) in Kansas;" *The Transnational:* "Postmodern Predestination," "Apartheid Pig Pile;" *PlaySpace:* "American Cheese;" *Syzygy:* "Seizure: 100 BC – 2015 AD," "Location, Location, Location;" *Ealain* issue 11: "All Is Fare in Love and War," "The Impressive Implosion," "ER;" *Big Bridge:* "MasterCard Detonating Charge;" *Whimperbang:* "Vision from Penal Colony for the Unemployed;" *Former People* "Cemetery Emissary;" *Bijou Poetry Review:* "Climate Change;" *Teaching as a Human Experience* (Anthology): "Class Time for the Arts"; *Brev Spread:* "How the West is One," "Sewing Machine;" *Harbinger Asylum:* "Class Time for the Arts," "The Next Move" *Nefarious Ballerina:* "Tinkered Tailor and Seamstress;" *Anomalous:* "The Clone Rhymes Now at Home;" *Write This:* "And We All Fall Down;" *Poydras Review:* "All that Is Might With the World;" *Eudaimonia:* "Dinner Time" (*Republication*); *Dark Sky Magazine:* "Whelk and Wealth;" *Negative Suck:* "Anthem Vent;" *Pemmican:* "Hearts in Heels," "No Change," "Okie Dokie;" *Trespass:* "Tuber Maneuver;" *Solo Flyer:* "Dental Record," "Get a Grip," "Shanks and Then Some," "Sole to Ankle," "Dinner Time," and "Country Folklore;" *St. Andrews Review: Cairn 42:* "Wet Nurse;" *Interpoetry:* "Calamity's Colossus;" *The Externalist:* "A Midnight Ride;" *War, Literature, and the Arts:* "No Cheating;" *Thin Air:* "The Mortar for Oblivion;" *Wild Quarterly:* "Skipping Poetry;" *Mad Hatter's Review:* "Returnables;" *Red Savina Review:* "Conspiracy Theory," "Prologue to the Impossible;" *E.Ratio:* "24 Hour News Cycle Spoke;" *The Montserrat Review:* "Gun Control;" *Reconfigurations:* "Complacency Report;" *Grand Street:* "The Forty Years on Essence;" *Niederngasse:* "Survival of the Fitter," "The Misnomer;" *Rio-A Journal of Arts:* "The Berlitz Fool," "American Elite;" *Pleiades:* "The Kiok Cop".

Body Politic
Rich Murphy
©2017 Rich Murphy

Published by Prolific Press Inc. Johnstown, PA.
ISBN: 978-1-63275-084-6
Edited by Glenn Lyvers
Assistant editor April Zipser
Printed in the USA

Contents:

For Bonnie,

whose companionship and support made this book possible, and to my editor, Glenn Lyvers, whose faith allowed me to share this vision with the world.

Arms

"For this I will demand to be respected, I'll persecute whoever does not show me respect. I live peacefully, I die solemnly – why, this is charming, utterly charming! And I'd grow myself such a big belly then, I'd fashion such a triple chin on myself, I'd fix myself up a ruby nose that whoever came along would say, look at me: Now there's a plus! There is a real positive! . . .

"It's a burden for us even to be men – men with real, *our own* bodies and blood; we're ashamed of it, we consider it a disgrace, and keep trying to be some unprecedented omnimen." ~Fyodor Dostoevsky

"Accordingly, with admirable, though misdirected intentions, they very seriously and very sentimentally set themselves to the task of remedying the evils that they see. But their remedies do not cure the disease: they merely prolong it. Indeed, their remedies are part of the disease.

"They try to solve the problem of poverty, for instance, by keeping the poor alive; or, in the case of a very advanced school, by amusing the poor." ~Oscar Wilde

"In our own time, the mechanical world picture at last reached the state of complete embodiment in a multitude of machines, laboratories, factories, office buildings, rocket-platforms, underground shelters, control centers. But now that the idea has been completely embodied, we can recognize that it had left no place for man. He is reduced to a standardized servo-mechanism: a left-over part of a more organic world". ~Lewis Mumford

"Since the end of World War I, the United States had devoted staggering resources and money to battling real and imagined enemies. It turned the engines of the state over to a massive war and security apparatus. These battles, which have created an Orwellian state illusion of permanent war, neutered all opposition to corporate power and the tepid reforms of the liberal class." ~Chris Hedges

"The conscious and intelligent manipulation of the organized habits and opinions of the masses is an important element in democratic society.... It is the intelligent minorities which need to make use of propaganda continuously and systematically." ~Edward Barneys

"(The world is profoundly unjust and must be changed, but the peaceful coexistence between American imperialism and the Stalinist bureaucracies, on the one hand, and the reformist politics of the European, and especially the Italian, workers' parties, on the other, are directed at keeping the proletariat in a subordinate wait-and-see situation that throws water on the fire of revolution, with the result that if the global stalemate wins, if social democracy wins, it will be capital that triumphs through the centuries and the working class will fall victim to enforced consumerism.)" ~Elena Ferrante

"Today, you'd have to cut banker's pay by eighty percent before their jobs were remotely comparable to other jobs." ~Zia Haider Rahman

Okie Dokie

From one end of Hoki-Poki to the other,
the desire denied and pain delivered
didn't pause for the Hopi.
What is Victor Vertigo to do
with washer machines and cellophane
for viewing domesticated animals?
In states that have tapped one spigot
for greed and charity, each dancer
participates in the grab or starve.
The music guzzles time while
the wasted folk frisk and shakedown
dervishes, theft and might.
Drum beaters distribute the party favors
well into the night.
While dead skin comes alive,
fingers point to a god
and so much loss opens a soup kitchen.
The obese wallets stagger and drag
themselves to the banks along river
Thank You. For the nickel miner,
the fortune revolution spins in the admiring.
Tricks find the hub of passion and need.
A plumber fine-tunes the instrument
for composition and show time,
and that's worth a holler about.

Location, Location, Location

"The first seal of Massachusetts Bay Colony showed a nude American Indian with a bush covering his groin. Like the current seal, he held in his hand an arrow pointed down. A scroll came out over his mouth with the words "Come over and help us", emphasizing the missionary and commercial intentions of the original colonists." ~Wikipedia

"The primary threat to US' interests is posed by radical and nationalistic regimes that appeal to the masses of the population and seek to satisfy the popular demand for immediate improvement in the low living standards of the masses and development for domestic needs and these tendencies conflict with the requirement of a political and economic climate conducive to private investment with adequate repatriation of profits and protection of our raw materials shares" ~Chomsky

Cash on pallets, guns
with something to prove

Lust arrived!

(Damn, smallpox didn't invade)

Pot-hole filler peace-pipes followed

Running Water also
once called through a green valley so
in a now alien country

Casino reservation or starvation
and alcohol rub

Lame Deer sends a "good luck"
to Afghani rug-makers

Soon enough wall-to-wall

and boom enough for some
upside-down hanging around

entrails from technology blanket
the trail to the 21 Century

Without consent and the pleasure
all hours without apology ever

Tourist traps take revenge
with kitsch, knick-knacks,
and quiet resentment

From outer space
one more Enlightenment patch
on Earth

No Cheating

"What I've tried to do all along here in this endeavor is take the rear view mirrors off the bus--and we have always tried to look forward, and that's where we are right now as well."
~Gen. David Petraeus

With the rear-view mirrors off the school bus,
the current event careens toward the end
for waiting children at the next pick up.
The classroom needs no brakes, and
its wheels whine about mocking
each generation meeting the road to nowhere.
The median between bravery
and fool-hearty wears the uniform tire tracks.
Bell-curve suspension glues faces
outside the lines to the ring and to disbelief.
Screaming tired from rubber, rules
and one-plus-one-more straight edge bully
prompt the custodian to the scene.
Bearing down on the chalk, bored to death
over the poor or less on the blank sheet,
the gym-grade student-vehicle climbs and plunges.
The only neighborhood past
whizzes candy by examinations.
Old calendars preach many sloppy Xes
to the promiscuous seeing-is-bereaving
orange assemblage speeding: where oh here
did the little dog go.

Recessed into seats or blurring glass panes,
snotty horror tells the trail once again
to Beau Peeps clutching their eyes
for roller coaster pride that dupes them
with lunch money for their tomorrow.

Ploughshares' Share

Business as usual: after each war,
farmers bury the meat grinders
to grow financial fields.
The rows to plow innovation
yield markets of trimmings and trauma
on the butcher shop floor,
but cow hands expect to risk
their cream and spleen.
Hamburger wheels itself through
ignorant citizenry.
Mail trucks deliver
battle scenes to the public
well after bull brains come home.
The rinds of poverty
have filled fry-olators
and bars of soap for millennia - Sow.
CEOs feed their franchises chicken feed
to keep the steers in the army chute.
From inside the clime and pace
of violent economies,
a column in a newspaper
once bandaged pork loin.
The letters may one day
blow their good health
across the future breakfast table
to soldiers of someone else's fortune.

Country Folklore

The beheaded government ran around
the barnyard squirting bullets and blood.
With the oven heating up, the farmer and wife
absorbed the violence and dressed dinner.
After the religious Feast of St. Loot,
the occupying army put its feet
up on the table and picked its teeth
until insurgents hear belching
and the coup backfired.
Sweetbread and neck bones boil in a soup
that has every liberated citizen treading broth.
How did the country with its range,
mountains, forest, and fields become
someone's recipe for just desserts?
What hunger do big shots aim to satisfy?
Questions grumble in the gullets
of herds and milkers.
Neighbors and folks from nearby towns smell
the quagmire stew of ambushes and convoys
and cross borders to the ladle.
Fools with explosive news
want a piece of the passion.
The new host and hostess
greet the parties with disaster.
Seats at the peace table need to be dredged
from a swamp of body parts.

All that Is Might with the World

Even in the commuter age drive
distributes hunger and coercion
to power the marginal
and main street pipe organs.
Livers and legs harmonize
resentment and dreams,
a hard swallow song.

The starving don't always want;
the wanton always lack.
Short-lived memory cards
grant mother boards towers
and the lucrative corporate circuitry,
while laborers fill holes with their bodies.

Tomorrow brings focus away
from alternatives also
and burns through pockets
of resistance. Dog whistles
divide what would have been
rabbits and churches prey.

Will and Frank Realty
thank their lucky Darwin
for their success and the slow
sand irritating the oyster prophets.
The choir has its pecking order
and nesting protocol also.

Afterlife needs no court
worming around estates.
The pigeons beaten, molested,
or neglected when children
can go to hell.
The bubble birds celebrate
champagne campaigns.
Aaahh - men.

Mortality Play

Before going on stage,
Mr. and Mrs. Marbles
pull on reason, tuck instinct
down around the waist band,
zip up emotion, buckle rationale,
and leave the house
with platitude on lips.
Sanity sets on the commuter rail,
nuts in a tube tip this way and that.
The altruists, Ringer and Dropsy,
sell precious moments
to collect cat eyes.
After the event, an alibi, the fish story,
circulates in a tank, the living room.
On news programs,
a parallel universe attempts
to kick in the front door.
Even with lessons learned,
new judgments inspire will
and torturers to use kitchen utensils
on owners again, and again
a morale compass will edify.

Subaltern Grief

The false consciousness chink
between brow and bridge
drapes ideological commitment
from peak to foot. For wherever
the breathing beneath the born flag
originates, this public skin grieves.
Ancient insecurity owns night and day.
The full face ignored
and then forgot the girl, wife, widow.
The open mind closed too early,
and so English lacks a hand to help.
Each letter here will never touch a veil
nor will a thought lift a woman
from the shadows and shroud.
The irony persists, however,
languages wait for the voice
stitched to body, woven alone.

Subaltern

From between lines,
the facts roll over words
to entrench themselves
before each sentence.
Boot-heel-crumple and
tank-tread-crimp sounds
cause laughter, a language
rushed into the forgotten.
Select truth zigzags
from one burnt out idea
to a bombed word,
letting possibility
until it bleeds
into easy concrete terms.
Generals in wind-bag bunkers
determine legitimate
from the platitudes
plied by the unemployed.
Underbellies edit stones from rocks.
The small arms fire
flickers among the distant hills
outside city mouths
emptying certitude
into the atmosphere.
Even the rural folklore
sets fallow, furrowed with craters.
For the rule of awe,
newspapers report objective
both barrels and blogs
into the options and innovation.

The inmate trapped in useless
cause clauses doesn't search
for the utopian weapon
to bomb the confidence
from the mean and raw confidants.
A pi piece peace, a share here there,
open fields would dew the desk pest.

Cemetery Emissary

The graveyard for empires
employs 24/7 pallbearers
who greet the potential
bereaved with Kalashnikovs
and RPGs. Hearses transport
foreign armies to affront.
Generals with heads sitting
on shoulders hit and run.
To stop guts risk for certain.
Headstones expose ambition
four miles high
and display engravings
where tribal cultures hole up
with supplies and running water.
The quagmire sucks on bones
from military vehicles
buried in depleted morale.
Air lifts gaseous remains
out from between valley walls.

How the West Is One

Against the cold and sun, the aborigine
on Earth wrap mind and body
in symbols. Hysterical tribes
ignore metaphors that involve nature,
the arch enemy, and leave behind people
rich in blanket. During the wars,
power plants spring up, the superior flora,
while automobile maneuvers
out flank the horse and stag.
Suburbanite warriors cower when
clouds storm the barricade and lights
go out. The provinces respond
to mow down climate, while hedging
wet weather with leaf-blower
and whetstone where only four seasons
tire. To survive, anything physical
owns human functions, heels,
or lumps for the suck from biology
to chemistry. The high priest
for a dry river bed won't embrace
the fishy affair because the splash
in the news doesn't reel current
events to a glass half full.
Performing rites for the falling
temperatures, the figures for speech
hang on to history by a simile.

Forbidden Fruit: For Heller

To heal the gap between
individual freedom and an order,
first responders dip cotton bolls
into chocolate.
With the nutritional value
printed on the box
cities square the peg.
Once the isolated apartment dweller
grows hungry enough,
no further thought engages.
When the scab falls into grace
the hermetic seal to culture
prevents questions and bravery.
Safety replaces escape on tongues;
surveillance brings parishioners to knees.

Phew and Fewer Complaints

Protesters relieve the politician.
The excuse against duty dances
round an issue so that everyone
can go home where TV cameras
roll through the ballgame.
The fetish for like-minded signs
and cardiovascular exercise
puts aside injustice for a while.
An empty box sits in a closet
visited by hungry women and children.
Consciences clear with coughs or sneezes.
The rituals for more than mercy
mark the place for change
if sidewalk solidarity
could take eyes off the picketing.

A tweak or duct tape and paradise
arrives in golf carts and dialysis
for the obsessed but distracted spectators.
The declining member numbers
organize the social party
that shakes fists with dice in them
in casinos and rouse the manager
from his rounds. But when guilt
begins a movement, the tribe gathers
to unfix a fixation ceremony.
Lawmakers lean out windows
to taunt for longer purification.

A Midnight Ride

The body politic squats on the fence,
stuffing ballot boxes every two, four,
six years threatening to fall this way then that.
From one side a donkey won't budge;
from the other a grey wall tips,
excavating the posts from their holes.
Wearing a shaving basin and shielding
itself with a serving tray, progress
fancies itself achieving its end.
Time blows hair back and out
of heads without the rolling cameras
of campaign contributions.
The hobby horse of bosses, whips,
and lobbyists filibusters a dime
for widows and orphans.
The poor know where they stand:
the overpopulated chimera stuck
in the mud of party politics.
Outrageous fortune of the few others soiled
the psyches of have-nots
with the vacuum of victor's spoils.
Jails wail with folk needing food
and helter-skelter shelter.
Yet the lousy clothing or growling bellies
cast their lots with General Will,
who high on a nation's petard,
demands a lead in the polls
and won't give financial losers
the time of day.

The fishermen of small change
reel and roil at corner betting machines
that tally an 'illionaire's love notes.
Without saddle, the Old Guard's straddle
of pickets, protests, nuclear tests, elicits
hoots and hackles from the distance of an enemy.
Perhaps one day the pumpkin of polemics
will grow nimble knees of stirrups and dismount
on two integral hooves into the fray.

The Mortar for Oblivion

"Somebody's gonna pick up a brick" ~David Simon

In chicken fat and corn syrup
the bottom line rubs noses
from whole neighborhoods,
and bricks don't fly.

Addicted to last pennies
and bling, pharmacies
on every corner wink
at young and old limbs,
and bricks don't fly.

For cities, prison and boot camp
substitute, end welfare creep,
and absorb jobless benefits
but bricks don't fly.

Money ignores need.
Purpose abandons buildings.
Despair fills stomachs;
still bricks don't fly.

Curbed by stateless, glass-eyed
financiers, debtors wear
leashes that choke resentment,
and bricks don't fly.

MasterCard Detonating Charge

The ingredients to the fuse-to-nowhere
include a visceral knowledge
that the history angel follows,
an ability to endure suffering and sacrifice,
and the need for distraction that Ss provide.

Once lit, few inside
the snow-globe for industry captains
close eyes, cover ears,
or duck behind money,
the one place for no need.

Outside, in the terminal exclusion zone
the ill, bothersome, and elderly,
any movers or shakers
hide in basements, invisible still:
chatter, chatter, chatter.

The S.S. Powder Keg bustles with commerce
when setting sail each morning.
And the moonlight hissing
quickly turns into Zs in boroughs and slums.

Two-stroke engines produce / consume,
produce / consume,
propel both worlds while manufacturing
ignorance and brutality.

Complacency Report

Hearts and minds find shelter in denial.
Ministers and Samaritans
rescue conscience from the street
and rationalization herds the flock
toward the holes in the sand.
The social services staff
and marketing execs donate cushions
that envelop pea or poverty
and from mother via the kitchen
piping excuses remembered from childhood.
The "Do Not Disturb" signs
point in all directions without an owner
or an ounce involved in the trouble.
Alibi, forgery, and "not me" finger the culprits
convinced that innocence fills shoes
from the neighborhood all around.
Willed-ignorance tints objects beyond noses:
Om sweet ohm.
Blame rains on the homeless if need be.

In other states, Libya or Myanmar,
mandatory amnesia and blinders
focus the population on freedom.
If a sense of self exists in the dogs
that populate domestic terror,
then lasers burn holes in propaganda,
ignite rebellion at any opportunity.

The couched position-statements
that fall from the malls and grocers
around democratic postures
escape an adult sovereignty.
The P.R. campaigns threaten
with discomfort food
self-served in a refrigerator box.
The false dichotomy economy plumes
larger than suburban life in the leaflets.

The Reign

Glasses containing salt water stand
for salutes, according to the Dalai Lama –
"Confusion, attraction, aversion."
The general air at the shopping mall
wavers between thirsty and quenched:
Attention brings an order to every day.
Marketing pastes eyes to Crystal Lake,
and coastal cities march to Utah.
"Parade rest" props for hip boot dreams.
Ah, addiction strategies at the outlet
permeate place and stroke each sense
nerve-ending with promises never met.
At the alarm, clocked for a toast,
withdrawal jitters until the engine
roars with insatiable sips, and the sun
steams drier with each gasp and gulp.
When the river bank gives way
and good credit washes toes, the bones
arranged lotus-style in the desert
advise with wry humors: A sky will fall.
No worries for the fund managers
vaulting teller stations and floating
in backyard pools playing with flutes.

Gun Control

The trigger lock for the rifled
end of his life is set and held
in the sight of both his pupils.
His world accepts the random beast

who would maul and wolf
his possessions, his moods.
His splinted index finger
points to the earth and blame:

all evil mixes with thin air
and rises to ribbons, shoes.
On his blind sides, the wilderness
waits its turn, his turn: Job.

Savaged at the wink of an eye
toward heroism on the "SS Lollipop"
or tested as a bored weapon unleashed,
he peeps through each dawn and focuses.

Climate Change

The corporate state plays
democracy while integrating fiefdoms.

The alarm numbs each subject
to fear while every charade
throughout the global prison
records weather on futile niches.

Using a canned laughter process
and a corkscrew, darker after-hours
drill inmates on buying a sunny day.

The Survival of the Fitter

The new tool balances weather's spinning
beach ball in the hands of the inventor
and renders improved devices
of amateur jugglers
jury-rigged broomsticks.

The instrument with myriad attachments
useless in the queue of pedestrian needs
overgrew the arms of manipulators.

As the engineers gather to witness
and confirm the simple control
from the planted feet of the innovator,
adjustments and enhancements
are added to the magic.

After the drunk driver on a crowded street
corner has owned the unassembled contrivance
a child's lifetime, the improviser
goes to work testing, implementing
the dream of a summer day near the ocean.

And We All Fall Down

The Big Other short-circuited blood ties
between itself and any body.
Yet cities light-up under
the estranged influence.
Siblings also long for the word exposed,
cower at father marching
in the dark between ears, and thank stars
for pockets filled with poesy.
The axis about which desire
and fear spin carries populations
upon paved language.
Tinkerers, innovators, and inventors tada
cash from the public
while a hand-basket delivers
such things as climate change.
Consumers need diets.
The gas pedal and brake
play a drum and then cymbal somewhere.
Green lures while surveillance
taps shoulders from behind.
The pleasure principle
and good conscience
leave commuters, tourists,
and the driven the billboard
and behind it, the police.
Even smiles cracked against feet droop.

Calamity's Colossus

Filled to its eyeballs with testosterone,
the utopian trophy stands just outside the city,
where citizens of peace and justice plot
its progress to their square.

The men of the town in their loose
horse-hair costume wait quietly for the orgasm.

But when celebration's cask spills guns and guts
around the laurel and brass, surprise
even grips the children.
Carrying a bucket of estrogen and a crutch
women respond with alarm.

After sexual domination's snow globe
empties, the scent of satisfaction
fills the air dressed in a promise of change.

Expectations grow greater and greater.

History's crystal balls,
hanging between the legs of biology,
bring Earth into focus.

Anthem Vent

Windsock suits TV and radio.
Trends where sunglasses and umbrellas
avail hands and ears, lend industry.
Gus gush spreads utter-butter better.
Oxygen lost shod stakes
among laundry on lines.
Sheet music propped in front
convinces the dancer doing a sidewalk.

Giving an elbow to the beggar,
carbon dioxide whisks the good air away.
Ecstatic with a kindness,
a breathless mob waits for orders
in a tunnel vision high pressure system.

When the storms arrive pledging,
aluminum panels and directing boards flap;
neighbors tax neighbors until
strangers pay in full for the rest.
The howl shows lungs how to vote:
bootstraps over shoulders –
even with boulder holders.

The jet stream moves freely
but balloons celebrate one direction.
Back in the day bogged down
in wells and thistles, sailors
huffed and puffed linen.
No different the broadcast
for bloomers one day
and for crossbones on another, the very next.

The Botch Banquet

"We are the sin-eaters. It means that we take the moral excrement we find in the equation and we bury it down deep inside of us so that the rest of our cause can stay pure."
~Bourne Legacy

The sin-eater field-day festivities:
The ends digest from memory
and the mean bottles

Company B arrives with chef hats on
and waitresses

Beagles into bugle-dogs for reward . . . but dog

The red-letter occasions, not rare but raw,
precludes by fare, fair:

Limbs in trees, roots rerouted, touted

Wolfing stomachs
while most intestines fail into lippage

Trauma pisses and pukes,
squirts out sides: a fast food catsup container
stepped on with a "huff"

Family and friends bleed
for food fighters and acrimonious weepers
to seek hospital bed prescriptions

The jubilee jamboree ekes to close
with meat-ends and shit on the table

.

Graffiti

A shaken can dew
on the stall
What rose stinks
Coal mine burying canaries
A code breaks over heads
Police batons on parade
Bulletin board bravado
CPR performed on PR
Front row seats fill
with engineers chirping consent:
The scoop
Law abiding citizens slapped with suits
and the few voters stunned stupid
Suites reserve for connoisseurs
whose perches creak
when can dues shakes

The Nation State

Day-to-day state violence
collaborates with the bottom line
to farm victims for cash,
and to intimidate restless thinkers
by tucking avengers into prison.
Before bed, global indifference
bubble-wraps, boxes, and
dividend-delivers the conscience
from poverty-stricken human
experience so sugar plums may dance.
Executive officers and beggars
never meet before or behind the eyes
that wage-earning, job-patchers
use to assess scraping together
what a senator wouldn't touch.
The prods, fraud, and banks remain
secure from justice and a social contract.
Furrowed-brow croppers give up
dollars to pass time on Earth.

United State

The failed state collapses to earth.
A hand from Western Europe on cheeks
and a cold sponge by Japan
on the body politic bring about
convulsion, shivers.
Joy, sorrow, mettle
disappeared into blank stares
too zombie to jail or flail.
Moods and attitudes
flee into basements
where guts have long hidden.
Locked from the inside,
catatonic folk refuse
with kicks and screams
the invitation to engage the world.
In the streets a tool with a hammer,
butt, and a barrel
cuts through traffic and points
out directions to targets.
Puppet masters string up
the walking dead for elected office
and Plato's cave-dwellers applaud.

As Enfolded in a Blanket

"You are just a human being, afraid, weeping under that
blanket, but there is a great space within you to be filled with
that love. All of nature can fit in there" ~Lame Deer

Enfolded in dearth until death,
great grandparents once cartwheeled
among the cycles that spun heavens and earth:
Unity dizzied with a comfort.

Last Deer engages in hand-to-mouth combat
on a reservation against cyborgs who beat
from dirt inroads for impulse.

The mechanical consumer-fetish demands
from the inspirable, the brand new
(or facsimile) for closet, attic, curb.
A computed-wardrobe repertoire, authenticity stages,
technology pinching to invent cheeks.

Geronimo, the cannon ball,
will splash for generations to kingdom come,
the hole in the country side,
wallpapered for mantels.

The broad-loomed earth absorbs also,
missing the mark, missing the people
fearless to face the presentation
by the sun, moon, and doom.

Tips About the Buttocks and Brain

In the one-room schoolhouse culture,
the parrot-or-stick order teaches.
Quick-study geniuses sing
the bars on the gilded cage.
The bruised and broken flee thinker
eats crumbs from hands.
Cookie-cutter kids grow
into ginger-bred men and women:
Watch what one says
to avoid the park benches;
ignore the touchy-subject warning
and burn in the neighborhood hell.
When the branch-shaker speaks
repeat from the birch perch:
Tell the ear what it wants to hear –
not the want that ponder has here.
No hurry to understand the command.
Over an educational career
the scholar gets to know the boss.
By then a pigeon hole nursing home
waits with assistant professor living.
The pointer and yard switch
outline facts and morality –
the grave and the grave
for the age to treason.

24 Hour News Cycle Spoke

Spinning for a living,
open wallets sneak around.
Dizzy constituent democracy suspends
before them who do and don not believe.
Where the wheel of the interpreters
and the audience meet:
Rubber road, tufted load, puff, poof, pfft.
At the sprocket
where the $5000 dish dinners
balance, clinking glasses
and the current events distract:
On the side of ignorance
the joke so few voters know
runs for election each term.
Pedals push back at talking heads
while the juggling exercises
at rights and lefts.
The viral blogospheres infect
with good senses of timing.
The handlebar mustache bell rings
but never crashes.

The Box Sets

"You become a prisoner inside all of these boxes."
~Lame Deer

In the prison without windows
tribal stick-figures interact on the walls.
Lexicons lodge outside under logs.
Market and PR recitation material
slide under doors at mealtime.
Every cell in the neighborhood
contained enough furniture for a castle.
Shackled to each other by finger fetters,
inmates enforce the gruel drool policy
to ensure compliance, the rules.
Born in captivity, any cub
squeezed into flesh from fools
embraces the same fate and makes a bed.
Alternative affairs live universes
beyond the halls, unimagined.

Cold-blooded air masses swept
wobbling bi-peds off feet,
so sturdy survivors went to war.
Beaver and raccoon ribbons
dressed the remote soldiers.
Jailbirds pasted reason on thin air
and on any trees left standing.

Shut-ins squat against blasts from heaven
and rearrange excuses for the source.

The Standing Joke

Should a brain survive
without corporate marination,
the troublemaker suffers
in exile away from the street.

The jingle lingo saturates
under hats until limbs act
the stage directions and fingers web.

Among mired minds where deep sleepers
bathe in the chestnuts and rubberstamps,
the commuter rides on slogans
that include coupons
for ignoring the elsewhere dweller.

Once limber, the latte sponge
cleans pop culture so that the fizz
in each bottled day titillates.

Templates and forms to pen
resources shape for the job
and the bubble-wrap champagne.

The grill upon which group-think roasts
for automatons and algorithms
chars into cortexes choking any reflection
with a proverbial glaze.

Conspiracy Theory

Syphoning willed-ignorance
and tweaking cellphone apps
manufacturers generate for the undead.
Lacking poetry, the production lines
spit from straight-faced university facades,
and middleclass shadows emerge with "yes"
on tongue tips and with dashes for legs.

Infiltrators laid in wait in banks
and at corporate headquarters
while insurgents poisoned
with pens 40 years ago,
experimented with group-think.
Sleeper cells embedded in Congress
to become lobbyists when called on:
Slow-motion jujitsu moves . . .
The welfare state rattled, riddled and rifled.
Elite brick and mortar forces
downsized into gas over cities, overseas,
to where the poor plunge.

Stunned and stunted by the crashes
on 9/11and 2008, the audience welcomed
into homes and on streets reality television.
And then the coup began
by co-opting fear and anger,
and spoon-feeding
to saturate keyboards, images, and ears.
Cliché and platitude propagated,
had long been for illiteracy coming to terms.
Shiny swinging objects and beds tether,
or armored cars mow – domestic violence.

The plot came to roil after debt enslaved.
The Corporate Media Awards Ceremony
rhyme at the Grand Ballroom
at The Caesar Palace in Never Mind, USA.

Across a Nation

The fright from Boston to Los Angeles
fills the cabin. No fight. War pinned
hungry volunteers with artificial limbs
and rooming houses welcome all
as the CEOs continue the globetrotting.
A rush among jobs to patch together
a living under cameras keeps the mob
from dwelling. The landing gear engages
the threats but not common ground.
Overhead compartments bulge
with worry. Beneath the plane
in the baggage hold, anger waits to be
unzipped: Marketing campaigns contort
and moralize for thieves. But as long as
fears outweigh each fastened safety seatbelt,
the greater community suffers need, greed.

Not (Only) in Kansas

Borrowed from offshore account owners,
billfold cash, savings, and credit cards
pause in transit from purses and pockets

The police may arrive in a moment
with shoplifting surveillance charges

or arm-twisting store clerks point
and the holder releases

Under the capital copula,
the huddled masses thank
while the consumption enforcement
officers rifle and rent among clothing

Burrowed between umbrella ribs
where the rainbow ends

when the productions slow at a dip,

a glimpse appears at the columns

that support with roles enough, Oh my

Notes from the Margin

The journey in the dark
from group-think to the dawn
where the desert continues
but without an envelope
around the mainstream
that promises quiet consent.
From the vantage point
where paying attention,
reading, and thinking converge
on higher ground, two eyes
watch corporations suck at nipples
in government barnyards
where taxpayers feed on garbage.
The thriving hybrid animal
in a deep state suffers
a military industrial complex:
Yike Ike was right
and correct with the warning.
A psyche for perpetual war
survives on processed news
and infrastructure scraps:
Gay rights, marijuana medicine.
Money mullahs pick ripe candidates
for the ignorant and privileged children.
Distraction drugs while drones dredge
the channel for empire.
The puny voice in the street
during lockdown waits
for rubber bullets and water cannon
until live rounds round the day.

Here corneas dwell, well,
and threaten ink on paper also.
The foundation and wish
may have helped compensate
for the genocide for milk and honey.

Junkyard Blues

The industrial revolution's smoking guns
sit cold blooded, still
pointing at the sky
next to the dead communities
who gathered for the drama

that would slaughter them.
The fingerprints reveal patterns of hope
by people of quiet desperation
who met knowledge only with use.
The nobility of feeding and heating mobs

led to drilling and splitting
for the mythic return to Eden.
Beneath tonnage of wood,
sheet metal, and plastic casings
each family's plot succeeded

in its scheme to steal more
than fig leaves for themselves:
in their pockets they stuffed their futures.

Greed ruled to reason every decision
until a market economy shot other possible
histories with cannons.

The rifled holes in the center
of cities and towns give witness
to the stitching of the continents
together by foreign children

now that the surgeons of privilege
have sprayed their atmosphere into truth.

The Clone Rhymes Now at Home

When the drones come home to roost,
dreams will be stuffed with "Hey you!;"
foxes will be detected in the cat
and mouse games; the hen house
will be bugged to determine
which came first the kitchen
or the egg; bedrooms will be projected
onto police station walls;
the wasps swatted by people
without business suits will trigger
the SWAT team; big brother,
hanging around every corner
lighting cigarettes, howling at girls,
and pointing out targets,
will mow families down
on backyard lawns; and remote controls
will motivate the idlers when standing
in streetcars or stuck in traffic.
The groans, heard from out of the blue
with perfect perch over shoulders
everywhere, don't whistle before explosions.

The Offensive Drug

With the white privilege needle
sharing veins, the pleasantries released
hide the blink response:
Black men fear black youth.

The unarmed desperate rage
riddled by white anxiety
bleeds out in the street
and sparks the unheard voices
who break windows and torch cars.

Even after 9/11, the insider strategy
needed every scapegoat in prison or dead.

Prosperity theology and the cool thermometer
drone on useless, elections, when a thermostat
heats to a thermostate in cities
robbed by corporations and banks.

The mistakes in school produced
elite cowards and race traitors.

Without the myth deployed
and running for the arteries
throughout suburban neighborhoods
downtown fires would lose the trope:
the hell and demon.

ER

"[M]ankind are more disposed to suffer, while evils are sufferable, than to right themselves by Abolishing the forms to which they are accustomed." ~Declaration. of Independence

A civic low pressure exhales hello;
shocks in the news beat empathy
from a heart;
a commute extracts enough bile
to drown a town:
The ideal survives on life support.

Outside the hospital,
fear swings a bauble on a chain,
and, going through motions,
workers run among jobs
in order to eat or pay rent.

Alarm muffles to good riddance
in a pillow to make way for traffic.

Cynics fill stadiums with the blame game
while obese desires grow vicious at supermarkets.

The creators and maintenance personnel
for group-think go about business
not taking any coercive advice fed to minions
(who don't earn millions).

The ill-health that ensconces
a broadcaster for public relation clients
kills the bitter and sweet lodgers
one-at-a-time, each staring at a wall in a room.

Phantom Limbs

"When plunder becomes a way of life for a group of men living together in society, they create for themselves in the course of time a legal system that authorizes it and a moral code that glorifies it." ~Frederic Bastiat

"[Habit] is the enormous fly-wheel of society, its most precious conservative agent. It alone is what keeps us all within the bounds of ordinance, and saves the children of fortune from the envious uprisings of the poor." ~William James

"The unending chase for money I believe threatens to steal our democracy itself. They know it. They know we know it. And yet, Nothing Happens!" ~John Kerry

"[M]any professionals, opinion makers, communications media and centres of power, being located in affluent urban areas, are far removed from the poor with little direct contact with their problems." ~Pope Francis

"It violates the essence of what made America a great country in its political system. Now it's just an oligarchy, with unlimited political bribery being the essence of getting the nominations for president or to elect the president." ~Jimmy Carter

"[M]ost of the gigantic sums of bail-out money went precisely to those deregulated Randian 'titans' who failed in their 'creative' schemes and in doing so brought about the meltdown. It is not the great creative geniuses who are now helping lazy ordinary people; rather, it is the ordinary taxpayers who are helping the failed 'creative geniuses.'"
~Slavoj Zizek

The Way Empire Ends

Psychiatrists around the time table
spread the cognitive map
for corporate generals.
The conspicuous unsaid
rules the state for the mind.
Check-points, PR detours,
and marketing campaigns
deploy credit card slaves
who never dwell while fiat, fiat
moves limbs using purse strings.
Soup kitchens dish up self-blame daily
to the dispossessed who were
out-sourced military responsibility.
Workplace democracy and the gold standard
threaten the bread and circus
with what-could-have-been.
Philanthropists lead parades to shelters,
anointing the streets with green confetti.
Having squandered moral conviction,
white ghetto renewal devours a heritage.
Reality TV instructs with relief.
Duty and public service
sleep in lethargy, in effigy.
Fed by bottom debt,
vested interests dress for all occasions.
The make-up artists for
political theater and pretzel-twisted
journalism avoid history and context
while Baby Boom progeny
wait with patience for the whimper.

Thinking Revolution?

"The storm irresistibly propels him into the future to which his back is turned, while the pile of debris before him grows skyward. This storm is what we call progress." ~Walter Benjamin

Living in a language where dry wall
and linoleum, ceiling fan and 2x4s
shelter verbs, especially to be,
the pragmatist possesses arms up sleeves:
Fears metaphor, owns guns.

With only an American Heritage Dictionary
public good can't break through
platitude, cliché, and surface emotion.

Ruffians shove common sense
down throats and listen for return:
Pauli wants a cracker.
The radical imagination gobbledygooks.

Meanwhile, CEOs privatize social justice
and judges parachute into retirement.
As a dime-a-dozen domination yawns
in a punishment state, officials issue
pain for food and shelter:
The self-sufficiency meter measures and metes.

Lacking vocabulary, dwelling on a house
defines the everyday revolution.

Get a Grip

The rebel of any number of fingers
demands creativity. Paintings by children
with tacks hang around the house.
Having descended the tree, the troublemaker
engineers tomorrows. Push button
technology makes life easier.
Using a pencil in a pinch,
the rock of pages steadies
the shaping of each letter and minds
each line of graphite.

The contrarian, who flicks his nose
before each fight, sticks out when alone though.
Hitchhikers use him as live bait. Drivers joke
about a Mr. Stubs or Tom
as the gang of four prefer to refer to him.
Emperors call him The Exterminator.

But no matter what our index or middle fingers
suggest, we plunge the one we find hard to love
into plum pie with all the poetry in our hearts
and the dikes in Holland stop leaking.

Set anything opposite the jackass of the hand
and mules sculpt the innocent bystander.
Chin in, chest out, the drill sergeant orders
the all-thumbs soldiers and gets their attention,
and if Napoleon and his revolutionary army
ever salute, we wave goodbye to the world
we have come to suck at.

Dental Record

Standing at attention until they fall out,
the rippers and gnashers greet and feast.
The white wall guard, warning of its reserve
of adrenalin and muscles to use it, welcomes
opposing armies as allies. But just behind
every two eager beaver diplomats, two canines heel.

Over coffee, tea, or alcohol,
and a bit of meat or crusty bread,
the United Front for the Preservation of an Independent
Person
wags its tail while it leaves its paws planted, oaks.
While the party wages on, the parties
draw new maps and review plans
slicing, dicing, and icing spoils.

Not until the sweethearts and their hard candy
form words of love and kisses
do they discharge from service a soldier here,
a spy there. An old person in a nursing home
tells stories of glory through broken ranks
to a child who doesn't know what to believe but smiles.
The civilized primate of chewing gum, orthodontia,
and sirloin steak parts his lips to show his back bone
that he insists with pleasure.

Shanks and Then Some

Calcium laws broken, bones bent
separating shins from thighs,
so that beggars would be
comfortable praying. The hinges
of supplication then march off
to the altars of marketplace
and battlefield where they fold.

Scrubbing kitchen floors
while playing horsy for rich children
who never grow up, the dog-eared foil
doubles over and puckers for a living.

The toy soldiers' limbs, too important
to bow, stand to witness the lame
(who are already down there) placing
their heads on the block.

Flesh's hydraulic crane that situates
scaffolding for crawling under beds
or for lifting a fallen comrade
begins its collapsing along the legs.
God's mechanical femurs for coal
and hole diggers of all mines fuels
well-fed joints for charges to nets.

Sole to Ankle

Balanced by a child's piglets,
the arches of Triumph that support
ovation's standing erect an adult
of five or six feet, each on its ball.

The view weighs on the pads of toes
where the earth writes its haikus
and then on the heels that dog the soil
with their ability to print and soon
leave impressions that the horizon
also fits upon shoulders.

The various steps in constructing
a history and its map lead
Napoleonic gestures that traipse
and trespass. Autobiography
and images of here and there teeter
this way and that seeking a cane.

The bases upon which a human goes
about daily life install themselves
into shoes of hunter and hunted
only to expose their resting on the butt
of their laurel and missed opportunity.

Dinner Time

The anaconda in the body doesn't chase
its tail forever, rippling away wastes of time
or go to hell when its lair begins to rot.
Begging to devour the whole world, now,
the sausage with teeth bares all.

Heartburn and frequent trips to the bathroom
slow the canines and thyroid.
Pissing and hissing, the corkscrewed chakra
pops open a desire while bubbles
of contentment fizz meditation.
A daschund naps around the waist
until a new goal that smells of steak
presents its challenge and the greyhound is off.

The garden hose's nose has no patience
for the aum, aum of indecision.
Minced meat pies cool on suburban window sills
while the inhabitants of inhibitions fulfill
by eating dust of the neighborhood creep
and striker. The Lincoln tunnel
from the log cabin reminds every zero
at the backbone of what a funnel and ramrod
can do. Obese boa constrictors miss
their dreams by an inch or moment,
but they own the junk bonds of bonbons.
Spine's tapeworm celebrates
its religious threat against doldrums,
and its rollercoaster ride out wows its ouch.

Tuber Maneuvers

Sticks and carrots move the stones
among the population that scurries
from one side of the road to the other.
The garden of price and pain
grows no knowledge carrying in branches
the promise of bliss. Eternal
rewards and brass ages united
the past and future in prayer
against the motivational sneakers
haunting lure and lash. Now and again,
sacks of dirt and pubic hair shirts
occupy the minds with chores.
The orange illusion one hangs
in front of one's nose has
its roots deep in the wishes
of a horse exposed to the switch
from trophy to weapon. Drives
cart the ass and the fox through fields
of energy and magnetism. Spurs and spas
turn the corners of anyone's back
day or night. Least resistance
draws the path into focus,
and the gnashing of teeth along
the route keeps even the hero
plodding until a stomach is full
when people hit the hay and disappear.

Hearts in Heels

His memory swerving his body to miss
a rut six feet deep,
the developed land's pioneer
mounts his hearth-on-wheels.

Vacationing a trailer park all year,
each unsettled family tours a narrow corridor
of rooms and eats and sleeps
within the commuter's rubber-tired routine.

Planting his feet one night in Yellow Stone
and one night in Seattle,
a neighborhood's gypsy, leaving an ivy lineage,
dances and sings along interstate expressways
two weeks each industrial year.

Aluminum, veneered pressed wood,
and toy fixtures, roaming's seat, home,
the middle class hoboes
warm their hands on over-heated engines
and spin on death's heels
at redevelopment projects.

Cheek Ruse

"...then there's the truth. And since when is that okay?"
~Eric Warren Singer

With one foot in the confidence trap
a second meal plants and uproots
to find a way out.
The prey for hunter and scavenger
owns the beating
from a Promethean heart
and the craft to cobble and hobble.
The democrat crises line up
beginning at the voting booth,
past the bias-triggered jaw,
and into the belly in beasts.
The whistler and mother deny
the cocky nature in bird song
but skip to light fantastic when wing
and prayer call for heavy lifting.
Even while a sky falls, oxygen
stocks rise, and the furrier feeds
people to an animal called
poverty, the snared don't sneer
but blow air past teeth: cheese.
No need to plan for a rainy day
or desert conditions, Mr. Smiley
meets the taxidermist tomorrow.

American Cheese

Staged authenticity folds at waists
for the cameras above the sidewalks:

Everywhere red, white, blue bows.

Pretty flops. Rehearsals for bedroom
passion and other calls from nature
show in the affect on characters.

Deadpan couples couple.

Bathroom slapstick straight men
chuckle then buckle.

Full slips into giggles for women,
no bananas needed.

Meanwhile behind the scenes
prompts prop and practice makes.

Immigrants hunger for a smile
while European tourists can't swallow.

No violence but violins: Smooth bows.

The audience in the director chair
scares with a boo; shepherds
with a loyal staff into the photo chute.

Wolves in sweaters on catwalks
through Miami to cemeteries.

The Kiosk Cop

Materializing at the malls,
the cosmic vision of fashion designers,
placed in tubes by ad-men,
are extracted by the myopic mob.

From the cathedrals of commerce,
where salvation is found on the backs of their priests,
the faithful merchandise mongers
drive steel into the hearts of sin.

Adorned in manmade innocence, the snake skin
behind the wheel of the automobile
feigns a martyrdom and with ketchup on its lap
withdraws to a prayer's shelter.

With the distant happening
all the time, the two bit actors
arrive propped by their backbones
and unprepared for the lack of science.

Witnessing the shoplifter
and the TV season's color,
the cold and hungry worker
cannot look up from distraction
to be mugged by his private possibility.

American Elite

Daily, your liver is found intact
on the face of compressed
language by democratic quills
and left plain English: offal.

At this syllable, grafted onto the sheer
side of a mountain by your wish
to feel alive, your eyes expect
the return of dull wits and obituaries.

At any melopoeia, a literal sky
could scoop your spleen for the river
of news ink in parking lots for gulls.
Upon a page from the voluminous

Urban / Suburban Sprawl, a token
filler is hand enough to pass stolen
light. The dead space and oxygen takes
your breath away between the buttes.

The Forty Year Journey on Essence

Deep into adulthood she sits
within a distant adolescent beauty.
The dented cheers and rusted cheeks,
having passed through pregnancies
and chocolate boxes, pretend, almost unrecognizable.
Responding in kind, the bald
and football-shaped and the town
of homebody queens wait
for their lives embedded in their children
to pronounce them dead: 1 - 2 - 3 - Bop!
Within the huddling single family homes
everywhere high school or college days
are extracted from a sense of security.
Called to the latest fissure by her mirrored face,
she mines magazines for the gloss and tits
and bathes that body in memories.

The Misnomer

The victim buries the dead enemy
with a bulldozer and spit, while waiting
for his stretcher ride through his prisoners,
to a bandage, and the Deed to Earth.

Comprehended somehow beneath the ignorance,
the bank of fog retreats once again
to the newspaper's cool silo.

Announcing the virginal declarations archaic,
the strumpet blaring "Gad Zeus" and "holy host,"
the scientist stretches the sheets
and puffs a pillow on a tradition:

The citizen frolicking into sleep is waked.

The neglected child of castles cocks
a smoking revolver over the bowed heads
of worshippers, while collecting the inheritance,
but the historian born on the bayou
and raised in a cloud continues
to perceive love's anthem.

The Other Relationship

Big Brother, Never There, encourages desire;
then shames execution. The coaching,
surveillance, and guilty verdict
drag tribute from the runt.
The prodigal son garners little favor,
goes bankrupt, unless the home-boy
falls from grace. So the name-sake
arrives at the occupied bedroom
delivering parental vacuums
and silky visions for an underling.
Once the bait buries a hook
a mama's boy, a daddy's girl,
sink teeth into a smile and misery.
Movie cameras, satellites, and spies
guide the lips to the good humor
merely as witnesses. N. T.,
the accountant in robes,
puts on the spectators
and condemns for communities.
Heart beats each day attempt to avoid
the family shadow that throws
the catch back into the barrel.

The Berlitz Fool

With the poor talker's alms
glittering silver, loaded, and in the palms
of weak thinkers, the proclamations of justice
by lead tongues sentence to death banks full
of intelligent witnesses.

Listen to me; listen to me; listen to me
is the vocabulary of the American city graduate,
having had his hands up on a color TV
until his lessons were learned.

Hunting for an ear that stands under the buckets
of random symbols in a forest where nobody hears
the trees falling, the wormwood chemist
becomes impatient toward the lip readers
and punching bags, and pumps
a translation from his butt's pestle.

Capturing an audience dressed in blue,
the poacher comes down from the top
of his lungs. He counsels a cage,
mumbling death threats to himself,
the pockets of his mind bursting
with an electrifying moment.

Sewing Machine

Time stitches contingencies
into patchwork until history
warms hometowns enough
for sleep. At each intersection
among segments a button reminds.
The unlicensed citizen attempts
to pull vignettes up over the head.
Nightmare spills into the streets
if granny with her pins
and needles waits long enough.
The tossing and learning
on the edge that weaves
now heaves panic to varying
degrees at arrogant survivalists
in full march. Puffed plans
and unmet destinies stuff
each scrap seconds lend.
Some seamstresses and tailors
prefer death day and night.
Other threadbare shiverers
can't close eyes or numb to guilt.
Yarn yawners need
the entertainment industry
to cover the news that props
a pillow to a tickle. However,
tucked in a trunk the old quilt
exposes remnant memory
to feet and wardrobe
for penetrating moments.

No Change

Her relationships range from doll
to dollar, and then her unexplored dreams
of self are draped in crematory passion.
The pairs of limp limbs she joins around

lunch tables also add, subtract, and spread
sheets, as money clip playthings.
Wire and hair, identities are hanged
at birth in closets, behind material gain.

Its pockets at home, the ATM comes alive
in an office, a real boy with a long wooden nose.
His deal with living rooms holds him
as would a bride until he dies: Frisk,

but don't touch me. The empty-headed house
of pretense shrinks for Alice to wear it
as a painter's smock. Until then, the family
prayer attracts no interest: in dogs we trust.

Returnables

The sardine cans
follow one another into the city
while a poet relaxes all day,
crosses your tracks, dots your landscape,
and if you read one of his poems,
you've read them all. "Come out,
come out, wherever. You are!"
The sardine cans
follow one another out of the city.
Your life is filled with a house and its tools,
saturated with olive oil and prosody.

Skeleton Key

"I must remember that everything that happens to me is my life." ~Antonioni

PR pros only refer to a rhyming
dictionary when harmonizing certain
neighborhoods with bankers.
Security deposit boxes punch holes
into the sky, so that blocks may gentrify.
Otherwise, firm hands on keyboards
and fact-checking attorneys on hand
set the snare drums
around personal desires
and beat so that arm-twisting
remains unnecessary.
When the bait breaks into jingles,
the lasso yanks the brat
and sweetheart to the gaffers.
The other exclamation points cheer
and together teach be flat or mute.
Once the choir forms and reforms
around long-term debt,
preachers quiet down,
the big-boy pants stop wheezing,
and work toward entering a foreign land
to take and own sings with ease.

Wet Nurse

Coercion compromises the air that lungs suck at.

Responses to threats stick in throats;

blackmail coats bronchial tubes and the diaphragm;

and intimidation fouls veins with bad blood.

With carbons plugging oxygen's nipple,
relationships cough, gasp, sputter spittle
upon license or contract. Negotiations
at the courthouse suffocate from infiltration.

Wrapping another planet
in another galaxy, perhaps,
love circulates on Earth,
a rumor or telepathic dream.

Mean breeding mutations
peculiar to this solar system
and human organs seep through business' pores.
The prey give up their sweat and food
to eat their animosity
beneath shovelfuls of resentment.

Weaned on each other's compulsion and taunts,
stunted survivors begin to bark
beta to alpha in the streets.

Tinkered Tailor and Seamstress

Girth to groin, jeans and genes face off.
Lawns and gnomes surround genomes,
threatening chromosomes with no ozone.

Construction goes up all around X and Y:
Easy access to women and guns for guys.
The dirty pants disgust lab coats draped
over mammary glands and hip bones.
Seats give otherwise snug fits and starts.

Whim buckles and bolts fate to zoo blot,
and the tag-team wannabe wallabies clown
round the deliberate steps toward
osteogenesis and procreation.

Yet revenge by the karyotypes zips
the swarming flies, and with the heat
brands the auras in fashion.
Pedigree and hybrid mutations pin lifestyles
to the periodic table until an uncle arrives.
The recessive syndromes surge
while free will environs withdraw
and both heap tangled in the body.

Chronic Experiment

Mad scientists think the brain shrinks
to a pea when distracted by a promise,
and once programmed to hunger,
the gastric juice factories drool.

To canonize Pavlov to god status,
market stooges trigger city-wide
wallet dumps at debt depots.

So saliva stimulators massage all sensors,
squeeze every tomato for IV-drips
from hides to a vault.

When psychic secretions arrive
in time on chins for the depository,

only depth perception by the dog factor
can undercut an expected reward for a bank.

The guinea pig saves the victim
from the vegetable garden
or owes each shock a prayer.

Class Time for the Arts

Marketing students make up
the poetry class ("once upon a time,
a classy student group took
creative writing by surprise…
the end"), practicing hands
at "confusion, attraction, aversion."
for selling serial boxes, television spots,
and computer popup tarts
for straight As. Robert Frost,
Langston Hughes, and Adrienne Rich
sit in corners facing the walls,
useless but for columns that point
at windmills with nouns.
The dunce cap sidekicks study how
to steal time from employers
and from other obligators.
Admen madmen promotions
unleash rhetorician pickpockets
onto city sidewalks and into suburban
shopping malls. At graduation
the underclass toasts survival
with salt water in flutes because
only breathing remains free.
The good for nothing sleeps
origami on websites, crumpled
sex in dorm wastebaskets.

A Financial Fix

The addict lies in wait
for the frontier prey,
where fear and humiliation
divide workers and the poor.
Bankruptcy risks in tribal regions
or in the genome laboratory
maximize potential overdoses.
And Welfare and Socialism
rescue the lenders with rolled dollars,
mirrors, and razors if need be.
The high produced by scoring
headlights and charging the expense
to the dear shuttles a body
in a yacht or Learjet.
No adrenalin in genius
beats a horse dead
with more life lessons:
Mud hut dwellers
become janitorial staff
-- the borrowers win also.
Should the stretch limo
appear to own an occupant,
the force in legal abuses
shakes the money trees outside
that commute to and fro.

Behind the walls with lenses
that trigger police,
one snorter can breathe in
saving accounts for a middleclass
neighborhood each day
and leave the refrigerator boxes
near dumpsters to fend for themselves.

Poetry Bin

The cliché day promises so
that a variation on the theme
frightens as spectacle. Safety first,
safety first, safety first.
A risk crafted by hand
unlike lacks language
for the conveyor belt manager
and will be handled by assassins
on a country road at an odd hour.
The mold droppings
around dawn and dusk
fall into the poetry bin.
A rolling pin flattens spontaneity
and improvisation into seconds.
A sleepy morning stretches into years.
Decades follow with a coma.
Hammers, wrenches,
and computer apps feed on lifetimes
with great thanksgivings.

Skipping Poetry

Slipping on habits, sliding on custom,
only an eye cleated for detail ensures
footing through the day so that a week
holds tomorrow in focus.
The morning ice patches challenge slippers
from bed to the front door when routine
maintains the slick conditions for sleepwalking:
365 bouts times 20, and the old flick
in the body fast-forwards four seasons
until skating glides into a cemetery gate.
With a pickaxe and ear muffs intent
braves the blizzard blowing,
"Go with the floe." A toboggan howling
with the undead breezes by Amie
Striver who clings to a brain-frozen love.
Such passion may plant a foot
one day, the only step that owns manual.

The Fun Funeral

The suffocated imagination
found in a corporate state –
stiff and staring – suffered
the efficient sciences
and smoke stack pillows.
A fresh image arrested
without ever becoming clear.
At the hospital, scholars
on Blake perform CPR
but the visions didn't respond.
The murderers escaped in clichés
with platitudes for alibis.
In a line up, a general idea
posed as the details,
and eye witnesses pointed fingers
at any sophisticated language.
Schoolmarms and fine arts police
drive right over the worn out
phrases that bury possibility.
Children sit in electric chairs
To learn not to rhyme;
stuffed-shirted cyborgs
leave home at age five.

Sci-Fi Ambience

To prolong sleep for the lullaby
audience that tosses between awareness
and denial, parents replace
security blankets with mentors
and practical goals. Tucked in snug,
mom and dad ride the planet with a snore
if the totems continue to hold tight.
Without question, generations age
and wish not to be disturbed,
button-down to assurance,
but greater infestation claims the terrain.
Honoring death by dozing all day,
the fetish followers recite
the only way in the world: Zzz.
Bodies without faith in human resource
excommunicate the zealot
from bricks and muscle.
Dormant populations reproduce:
Creed creatures multiply and memorize
$$$ with flash drive and shortcuts.
Struggle loses definition,
becomes flabby, and selves
never get worked out.

Enlightening the World

Under the dominion dome,
privilege showers upon democratic suppliants
while weather outside saps and zaps

Where tents, hovels, and mud huts once promised,
now an explosive climate heaves
around families, tribes

The bubble bath illusion,
threatened by clan men, vaults
behind science and stakes for resources
behind refugee crisis and genocide

Wards-of-the-state washing armpits,
in no position to accept with responsibility,
deny to maintain advantage and flow

Chocolate bits, bandage dispensaries
quell around the heart in matters
when pursuit for happiness, instant please,
and the smiley face demand

Where natives stir restless,
an ore store begs to a CEO and diplomat
to be opened for business ...
and the cheat goes on

The mirror hurts in the eyes cynical
until a new nation acquiesces to the syphon
and the deranged dream for salvation

Easy chairs then hold for the pattern to end

Shame Game

Swimming against fingers pointing,
the beast of burden gets carried away
to meetings with fists and swept
into a boat alone. The small hole
in the frequent bow brings disaster for sure.

Beneath strange steamer trunks
and mislaid baggage,
the mule clutches foreign cores
to claim the incline into acceptance.
Piles of garbage draw teenage boys
to target practice, and clubs
beat a loner every time.

Big blame hunters safari monotony
for difference. The hump back
desert taxi swallows the hard
resentment at dry oases,
but never drops from the empty promises
welling camaraderie. The tips
on shoes also need licking.

Spittle from the lips that surround
form on the ox hide that cannot escape
the goat feet. Absorbent cloths cover the shun
and turn with stones. Born to sip back
blood with guts so that the death deniers may be
surprised by theirs, the elected
owe-it who staves off demise,
corners a logic that scares calm calamity.
The 0et in America could join the mobs
if only the straw man didn't echo
inside billionaires.

Whelk and Wealth

Oligarchs fill the rusty cities with lobsters
and watch clumsy desire flop desperate.
For propagandists silver pails brim
with shills with heads in the sand.

When architecture fades, designed containers
limit to the lowest crawls on Earth.
Sport fishermen give gospel on miracles
involving crustaceans culling the buckets.

Pity keeps a dry eye as the salt water licks
sure and rocky chops nearby.
News casters wear bibs for the butter
and sea brine that drips down chins.

Moving in for the krill,
the sharks long ago fixed sites
for bottom feeders and the maimed.
High schools police the hulls and hulks
for shells threatening the rim.

In the case that tenants
on city blocks didn't find prawn
in their cribs, pawns flooding the hood,
the claws weighing on shoulders
should have collected attention.

Trapped from paycheck to paycheck,
stones with life in them find reason to stir
even though they signal one for the boil.

Apartheid Pig Piles

The disposable people sit on the curb
behind the capital club where interest
drops off immediately:
10% - irrelevant in a second.
Derelicts and unemployed bodies
throw the human husks, breathing,
into the truck bed and return
to the dumping ground.
The bull session members
and bear huddlers own the math
that determine an 80% excess
in workers who may need stepping over
if not cleared from sidewalks
outside banks, below high rises.
"All nonessential employees
please report to the garbage heap.
Replaceable contingent personnel
hang around in line by age."
Predestination police cordons off
whole neighborhoods at pubescence.
Superfluous countries accumulate the trash.
Planned obsolescence determines
the value flesh possesses (with a snort)
as opposed to natural resources.
Newspaper pack rats earn caricatures
in the press on sidewalks.
Cat ladies imprison the caretakers.
But the dispensed with majority
sit blamed by role model money hoarders.

Seizure: 100 BC – 2015 AD

No one rules nakedly.
Myths and lies worn
for robes and vestments,
two ham distractions for shoes
permit for citizens
who remain children.

Diapers and rattles hold
to distance, and death
also seems to refuse an address.
Obedience freezes
so the indebted democrat stands
shoulder to shoulder to freedom.

The rod not spared
and threatening quiets
to graduation in the schoolyard.
Group-think tailored
for local leaders and statesmen
was woven from grade school
and television shows.

Throne for wolves,
ingsoc snares laying platitudes
alongside comradery;
then tickles with deep sheep.

Packs pounce from police stations
onto strays: dogs not kenneled
in one mirror-less attitude.

Closing in on the exile and hermit,
flash mobs and a growing consensus
suck from the air
and squeeze along borders
until the laurel refrain.

The Impressive Implosion

The inner-life demolition experts
arrive to work early.

Shells functioning without:
Each husk ceiling without
a sluggish Angelo to paint.

The ball to bat pitches from the womb.
Bases and a place serve up
underhanded from bottoming America;

the joke at school remains detonated
while a brain and heart reverberate.

Family and friends using ice cream scoops,
marauding police gangs
wearing stunning uniform cameras,

and disciplinary institutes
that apply tourniquets to psychic wounds
to shave for drumming
growth beyond a corporate state.

From ice pick lobotomy
to empty pre-fab storage facility
where the unaware façade
doesn't recognize the need for a resident,

the narcissus progresses.
Suns found in parental coat pockets
encourage pinning back
the wings on the city to remind

the subject and the drunken, resilient
question mark behind the eyes.

Vision from Penal Colony for the Unemployed

Where money earned in sleep
draws a blueprint,
systemic disinformation
offers up for "news" dinner:
Bad apples satisfy, fill.

Manufactured apathy manipulates;
engineered culture ignores,
but unfolding the map,
the good cognitive scout
can signal where distractions dangle
to camouflage the predicaments
and the right questions to ask.

Social justice commandos
struggle against international terrorism
at home; arm-in-arm citizen-raids
unearth again and again.
The entrenched deep state persists.

Delivered by local police in armor,
the non-pliable workers occupy
within walled streets.
The fiat-scrambled FEMA camps
for interns employ to shave into slant, spin
with razor wire that prevents
the coming democracy.

Disposed to suffering more
than to make right by abolishing,
the scapegoat and patient wait
for invisible hands to lift together
to oust the puppeteer for the sharer,
the black hatted magician for an orchestra.

Postmodern Predestination

At the frame shop for possibility,
what amateur artisan builds borders
around false choices?
Mats and mounting force adoption
to construct adapters?
One doesn't need to be a picky person
to participate without desire for the prize.
Right angles, seldom achieved,
end with minimal inclusion,
offer redundancy but no alternatives.
Any excess limits options to none.
With the winner predetermined
canvases collapse capture passersby.
To adjust requires events in a chain
that shackle the reconciled to submission.
The fable for freedom encompasses
but dumps the contents for amnesia.
A vending machine promising variety
dispenses the unwanted
without representation:
A politician steps from the tray
but slips into a back pocket that collects.

All Is Fare in Love and War

When banks rumble
into the village square
with turrets adjusting how-itzers,
crowd-easing machine funds,
and investment thud craters,
the democrat applies
to polish wing-tip shoes.

The IMF points and livelihoods
for wallets, hostages give up
in exchange for consumer handbooks:
Works for workers every time
at any rate.

The invasion acquires
through intelligence, sabotage,
and peace offerings
so that hands without weapons
move for the looter
around mines and sweat shops.

Chained to debt, a small business,
family farm, and laborer spread eagle
as colonizers instruct
with "heave" and "ho" for free.

Once the cognitive map unfurls,
the newly minioned cultures
celebrate privilege around
half-full water tanks.

Lullaby for the Lullaby

"And people flock around the poet and say: 'Sing again soon' - that is, 'May new sufferings torment your soul but your lips be fashioned as before, for the cry would only frighten us, but the music, that is blissful." ~Kierkegaard

For marketing campaigns,
mantra poets calm
before, during, and after
wallets empty and worse.
Sorry Mr. Ginsberg, the mystic
squeeze box vortex fits well
between yawning sex and violence; listen.

Pound pronouncements pounced in Pisa.
Abracadabra Rimbaud disappeared in Africa.
Logy yogi Whitman bought with spirit:
"Co-creator of the unintended."
(Maybe, Howl brought to balance Yawp.)

Snuggle up to Om in a new home
not owned for 30 years
but indebted to unknown suffering by others.

Sops for moral outrage
clean up where frames, lures,
and sugar plums entered
into public dreams without inspiring
the appointed behavior.

Should poet pain stop managing
at the life-long hospice,
having to pick rose petals from over eyeballs
could cease and the pencil behind an ear
could catch-up, could win.
The work toward waking
to owning a body may begin.
No one with a breath escapes.

Pluck at the feathers from the song
to expose the right questions
for the birds in the trees
for the dying generation.

The war may be lost
but integrity engages in struggle
to breathe through psychology
with places for heads to bump,
with rough ledges for gluteus maximus,
and with cause for the heart.

Hominid preying on hominid
whine on knees before posterity
laying claim to heroism and innocence.

Prologue to the Impossible

In the suspect society,
democracy implodes,
and, to create a black hole
for morals, willed ignorance
denies the violence.
Short term interest
for short term gain
erases memory, history,
and solves problems
using prison, better yet guns.
"Against the wall and spread 'em."

Corporate thinking manages:
Public issues efficacize
into private suffering.
The cheerful robots
who studied, practiced,
and blame themselves
own foreclosed hopes
and death urges.

Broad social justice movement
breaks into departments:
environment, race,
immigration, war, taxes, etc.
The boutique activism
provides overtime
opportunity for cops,
one weekend a month,
sometimes two and little else
where trembling shrinks men.

The impossible remains
on the storage shelf
in the basement, down
around the belly,
the only option
and nothing to lose
but fear.

The Next Move

Just before spontaneous acts
on a busy expressway
judgment may fork left or right
where any brush with weeds
alienates and authenticates.

To maintain asphalt and order
on the jaunt to the cemetery,
social authority and peer pressure
urges lollygagging and rewards
with salt water in a cup.

Along the roadside the interpolators
(some with chairs) cheer on
the lemming parade who in suits,
ties, skirts refuse the open fields.

The alternatives to the passing
lanes to death zip pants and scythes.
Where least resistance leads
may bring pleasure but freedom
packs a Prometheus most for the slog.

Published by Prolific Press Inc.
Johnstown, PA
http://ProlificPress.com